THE BOOK OF BOK

Written by
NEIL ARMSTRONG

Illustrated by
GRAHAME BAKER SMITH

wren
&rook

When I was a boy, I dreamed I was
high above the Earth with
only clouds for company.

For as long as I could hold my breath,
I floated.

But I could not hold my breath for ever.

I'd wake and watch the Moon drifting by my window, wondering at all it must have seen and imagining how it was made.

I learned that when the Earth was very young – four-and-a-half billion years ago – it was involved in a great celestial fender-bender.

A smaller planet smashed into Earth!

The collision sent billions of tons of molten rock into orbit. Over hundreds of years, this rock merged and stuck together to form a sphere.

The Romans called it Luna.
The Greeks, Selena.

We call it MOON.

It was a turbulent and terrifying time for the Moon.

Lava flooded up from below its surface, filling giant craters like hot soup in a bowl. Geysers of erupting gas shot globules of molten rock into the sky.

Half a billion years of chaos passed before the Moon began to quiet down. As the crust cooled, it cracked.

A piece of fresh young basalt **broke off** from a larger rock and rolled away.

I call him

BOK.

Geologists – people who study rocks –
have a saying: "Rocks remember".

History is recorded in the minerals and
marks of each boulder and pebble. During
the next four billion years, Bok would see
and remember many things.

He saw the Sun rise in the east and parade
majestically across the sky to set in
the west.

Occasionally, new stars would burn with
a fiery brilliance against the velvet
blackness of space.

Constellations changed their
shape as stars were born,
burned for millions of
years and disappeared.

Back then, the Earth also
rose and set.

600 million years

went by and then an asteroid struck Bok!

It **catapulted** him into the sky towards a crater at a terrific height and speed.

Bok held his breath for as long as he could.

But eventually he fell.

Skipping a time or two, he came to rest on the rim of a small crater. Part of his right side broke off when he landed. All his basalt neighbours were left far behind. He didn't know if they had been vaporised, melted or blasted far away.

Bok was **alone**.

It took him about half a billion years to get over the experience and settle down before, once more, turning his gaze to the sky.

Continents would creep out of the sea, **linger** a while and then slip once more below the waves.

And swimming **deep** beneath those waves was the **teeming**, earliest complex life on Earth.

Another billennium went by.
The Moon was quiet now.
Nothing ever happened.

But on Earth, plants appeared on land. Amphibians developed, ventured out of the sea and, in time, learned to live above water.

Dinosaurs roamed the Earth. But they disappeared almost before Bok noticed them.

An entire chapter of Earth's history.

Been and gone in the blink of
170 million years!

Bok was then a little over three-and-a-half billion years old and starting to feel sleepy.

Through tired eyes, he glimpsed the rise of the mammals. He saw the Earth turn into a giant snowball beneath the grip of the Ice Ages.

Just before sleep enveloped him, he saw a new creature standing on two legs, holding a flint-tipped spear...

...staring in wonder at the Moon.

He slept deeply as the Moon continued to accompany the Earth on its endless journey around the Sun.

And so he missed the unfolding story of humankind.

He missed Plato and Hypatia.

Charles Darwin

and Maria Mitchell.

Konstantin Tsiolkovsky and Bessie Coleman.

He missed the **birth** of the boy who grew up to climb aboard a rocket destined for **the Moon.**

Bok couldn't have guessed that his nap would end with a **rude awakening** early one lunar morning.

A peculiar creature was lifting him with an unusual metal device.

He was roughly thrown into a box with some acquaintances he knew only slightly.

Then the lid was closed
and it was dark.

Then a sense of **weightlessness** for a time.

Bok felt a brief force.

Flames outside the window blotted out the blue of the Earth as the space capsule streaked through the atmosphere, blazing like a comet.

The heat stirred a deep and ancient memory in Bok.

A memory from so long ago it seemed like a dream.

He remembered the early days of the Moon. The chaos and fire of its birth.

He remembered... he had been a part of the Earth!

Millions of people all around the world were watching.

Holding their breath until they saw the space capsule floating beneath three bright parachutes splashing into the arms of the ocean...

...returning all on board safely to the place from which their journey began.

And now you know some of Bok's history, you can go and see him at a museum in the USA – or at least a part of him. A chip off the old Bok, you could say!

Perhaps you might try and imagine what he is thinking as he looks out at us looking at him?

Does he see us as something new and different on this Earth that he's watched for so long?

Or, like the dinosaurs, just another species that exists for a brief moment of geological time?

After all he's seen, Bok must be very wise.
But if you ask him about the Egyptian pharaohs,
don't hold your breath waiting for an answer.

He missed them!

The Moon

The Moon has fascinated us for as long as we've been in existence. It is Earth's only natural satellite – the only object that orbits our planet that isn't man-made. Although it spins around just like the Earth does, we always see the same face of the Moon – because it rotates in exactly the same time as it takes to orbit the Earth.

Many scientists believe that the Moon was created around 4.5 billion years ago when a planet roughly the size of Mars collided with the Earth. The impact sprayed rocky debris into space, which eventually gathered together to form our Moon. At first it was very volcanic there, with lava erupting all the time. But over millions of years, things settled down and became quiet. The only disturbance was whenever an asteroid or comet struck the Moon, creating impact craters that we can still see on its surface.

The Earth

Our planet is about 100 million years older than the Moon, and formed when smaller rocks collided and clumped together. The impacts created a lot of heat, and for a while Earth was a boiling ocean of lava. But eventually things started to cool off, and a crust formed on the Earth's surface. Water vapour escaped, and soon clouds gathered. As rain started to fall and meteorites containing water impacted Earth, the crust was flooded, creating oceans.

The first life on Earth were very simple organisms that developed about four billion years ago. They evolved into much more complex life forms in our oceans and, eventually, on land. Dinosaurs appeared about 247 million years ago and dominated the planet until some kind of catastrophe. Most scientists think a massive asteroid crashed into what is now Mexico.

Mammals started to evolve in new ways when the dinosaurs died out. *Homo sapiens,* or modern humans, first walked the savannahs of Africa around 300,000 years ago.

Since then we have spread across the world and learned a great deal, thanks to ingenious minds like philosopher Plato, mathematician Hypatia, naturalist Charles Darwin, astronomer Maria Mitchell, pilot Bessie Coleman, rocket scientist Konstantin Tsiolkovsky – and even the first man to walk on the Moon: Neil Armstrong.

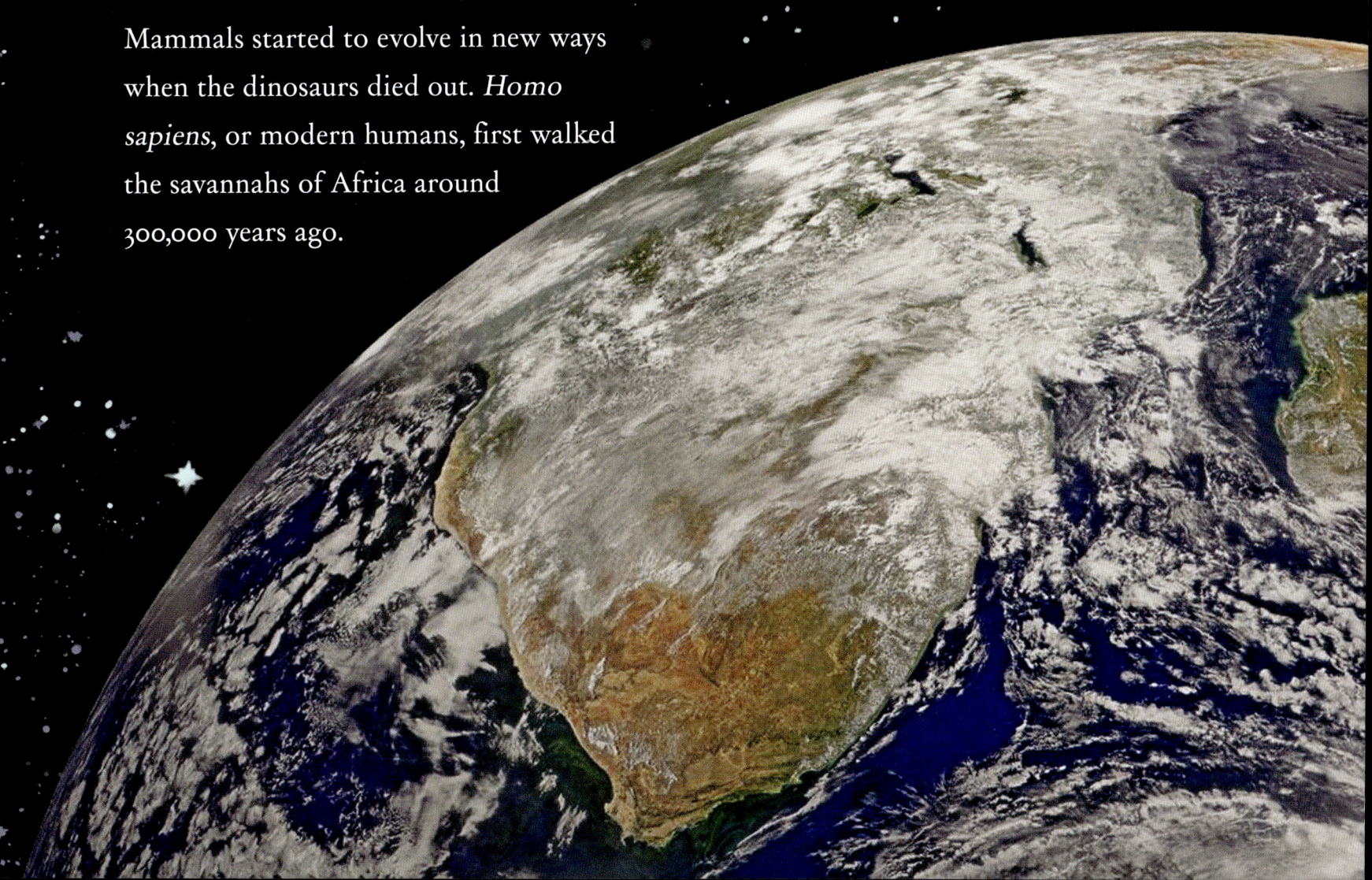

One small step...

Neil Armstrong's journey to the Moon started long before he climbed aboard his spacecraft. Born in Ohio, USA, in 1930, he first fell in love with flying when his dad took him to see an air show – and by the time he was 16, he'd got his pilot's licence.

After attending university and flying in the Korean War, Neil became a test pilot, flying all sorts of cutting-edge planes as they were being developed. But Neil wanted an even more exciting challenge than that, and in 1962 he applied to NASA to become an astronaut in the space program.

In 1966 he piloted the Gemini 8 spacecraft, achieving the first-ever successful docking of two vehicles in space. But minutes later, the two spacecraft began to spin wildly – and Neil saved the lives of himself and his crew when, while under enormous G-forces, he wrested back control.

Safely back on Earth, Neil was put in charge of the Apollo 11 mission, joined by two other astronauts, Buzz Aldrin and Michael Collins. The USA and the Soviet Union were in a race to try to land on the Moon first.

On 16 July 1969, Apollo 11 launched from Kennedy Space Center in Florida, USA. Four days later, having orbited the Moon 13 times, Apollo 11's lunar module set down on the Sea of Tranquility – which is actually an impact crater filled with basalt rock, not an ocean.

On 20 July, Neil became the first person to walk on the Moon, with 600 million people watching on TVs around the world. His first words were:

Together, he and Buzz spent 21 hours on the Moon, collecting rocks to take back to Earth for study – including Bok.

The crew returned as heroes on 24 July 1969, splashing down in the Pacific Ocean in Apollo 11's command module.

"That's one small step for a man…

…one GIANT leap for mankind."

In 2006, NASA announced Neil as an Ambassador of Exploration, and presented him with a small fragment of rock he had brought back from the Moon. During Neil's acceptance speech, he gave the rock a name – Bok – and imagined all the amazing things it must have seen throughout the solar system's history. Neil's wife, Carol Armstrong, had the idea of turning it into a book, and this is the result. Bok is now on display at the Cincinnati Museum Center's Museum of Natural History and Science in the USA.

First published in Great Britain in 2021 by Wren & Rook
Original Text © 2006 Neil A. Armstrong Trust, Carol Held Armstrong, Trustee
Original Text by Neil A. Armstrong, 18 April 2006
Adapted Text and Illustration by Grahame Baker Smith
Text Adaptation and Illustrations © 2021 Grahame Baker Smith
and 2006 Neil A. Armstrong Trust, Carol Held Armstrong, Trustee
Design copyright © Hodder & Stoughton Limited, 2021. All rights reserved.

The right of Neil Armstrong and Grahame Baker Smith to be identified as the author and illustrator of this Work is asserted in accordance with the Copyright, Designs & Patents Act 1988.

HB ISBN: 978 1 5263 6227 8 | PB ISBN: 978 1 5263 6228 5
E-book ISBN: 978 1 5263 6229 2 | 10 9 8 7 6 5 4 3 2 1

Wren & Rook, an imprint of Hachette Children's Group, Part of Hodder & Stoughton,
Carmelite House, 50 Victoria Embankment, London EC4Y 0DZ
An Hachette UK Company | hachette.co.uk | hachettechildrens.co.uk

Publishing Director: Debbie Foy | Managing Editor: Liza Miller
Art Director: Laura Hambleton | Designed by Barbi Sido

Printed in China

The publisher would like to thank the following for permission to reproduce their pictures: p 36–39 NASA; p 38 Purdue University Archives & Special Collections. Every effort has been made to clear copyright. Should there be any inadvertent omission, please apply to the publisher.

No part of this publication may be reproduced, stored in a retrieval system, or transmitted, in any form or by any means, without the prior permission in writing of the publisher, nor be otherwise circulated in any form of binding or cover other than that in which it is published and without a similar condition including this condition being imposed on the subsequent purchaser.

Early sketches of Bok